Golf:
It's Just a Game

The Best Quotes About Golf

Selected by
Bruce Lansky

m Meadowbrook Press

Distributed by Simon & Schuster
New York, NY

Library of Congress Cataloging-in-Publication Data

Lansky, Bruce.
    Golf, it's just a game : the best quotes about golf / selected by Bruce Lansky.
        p. cm.
    Includes index.
    ISBN: 0-88166-248-8 (Meadowbrook). — ISBN 0-671-57049-8 (Simon & Schuster)
1. Golf — Humor. I. Title.
GV967.L32 1996
796.352'0207—dc20   96-1098
                                                                        CIP

Editor: Bruce Lansky
Editorial Coordinator: David Tobey
Production Manager: Amy Unger
Desktop Publishing Manager/Text Design: Jay Hanson
Electronic Prepress Manager/Cover Design: Linda Norton

NOTICE: Every effort has been made to locate the copyright owners of the material used in this book. Please let
us know of any errors, and we will gladly make any necessary corrections in subsequent printings.

Cartoons: pp. 4, 34, 41, 85 © 1996 by David Harbaugh and *Golf Digest*; pp. 7, 95 © 1995 by Bob Zahn; pp. 15, 31, 52,
102–103 © by Lo Linkert; pp. 22, 49, 66 © 1995 by Joe Kohl; p. 44 reprinted from *The Saturday Evening Post* © 1990; p.
59 © 1994 by Jimmy Margulies; p. 63, 98 © 1993 by Lo Linkert. Reprinted from *Golf Fever* by permission of Spectacle
Lane Press, Inc.; p. 72 © 1994 Playboy Magazine; p. 78 © 1995 by Roy Doty. Originally appeared in *Golf Digest*

Poems: pp. 5, 25, 37, 45, 50, 92–93 © 1996 by Ned Pastor; pp. 8, 42, 75, 97 © by Richard Armour; p. 69 © 1996 by
Timothy Tocher; p. 83 © 1996 by Lois Muehl

Published by Meadowbrook Press, 18318 Minnetonka Boulevard, Deephaven, MN 55391.

BOOK TRADE DISTRIBUTION by Simon & Schuster, a division of Simon and Schuster, Inc., 1230 Avenue of the
Americas, New York, NY 10020.

01 00 99 98 97 96   10 9 8 7 6 5 4 3 2 1

Printed in the United States of America.

CONTENTS

ACKNOWLEDGMENTS

We would like to thank the individuals who served on a reading panel for this project:

Jerry Alch, Mike Arne, Robert Baird, Mike Ballard, Esther Bloch, Phil Bolsta, Patrick Bouyer, Jim Brockett, Dr. Hale Burnside, Bruce Candlin, Maureen Cannon, Ron Caton, Linda Cave, Gail Howard Clark, David Collard, Clyde Cooperman, Charlie Cornelius, Tom Courage, Dave DeFontaine, Ellen Dehaven, Jeffrey A. DeVano, F. Blaine Dickson, Peter Dominowski, Paul J. Driscoll, Mike Duncan, Ivor Durham, Bob Elkins, John Foote, Greg Geleta, Bill Gildea, David Hamdorf, Jay Hanson, Todd Harriman, Dick Hayman, Larry Holgerson, J. Hoskins, Karen and Bruce Huck, Bob and Joan Hursh, Bill and Dave Jadlos, Tony Leto, Ken Little, Trevor Lloyd, Tom Major, Barbara Mayo, Neil McEvoy, Vicki McKinney, Brenda Michaelson, M. Michellich, Lois Muehl, Sheryl Nelms, Jonathan Nelson, Brad O'Hara, Dale Owens, Dennis Pascale, Ned Pastor, Dave Paulson, Eric Peterson, Gib Poiry, Patsy Price, Art Scott, Bob Simmonds, Bill Skoglund, Joseph Taylor, Linda Torres, Dave Tutelman, John Vander Borght, Marvin Wallace, Ed Whitesell, Pat Wickham, Ron Williams, Bob Zahn, Seth Zimmerman

INTRODUCTION

I've been a double bogey golfer since I was a kid, but last January I made a resolution to break one hundred consistently. I took lessons and practiced driving, chipping, and putting. I played golf five or six times a week. I practically lived on the golf course. And when I wasn't playing golf, I was reading every golf book I could lay my hands on.

I wish I could honestly say my handicap went down significantly. But my game did improve in one very important respect: golf became a lot more fun for me.

In addition to becoming a student of the game, I became a student of golf humor. I began writing down the funniest things I'd heard and read. By the end of the summer, I'd found something funny to say about any situation: a hook, a slice, a whiff, a two-foot drive, a blown two-foot putt—you name it.

Hacking my way around the golf course gave me ample opportunity to try out my one-liners, and to collect more (on the back of my scorecard). I made lots of new friends. Even low-handicap golfers would invite me to join them in their foursome or for drinks after a round.

In short, instead of agonizing over blown shots (or swearing), I would use them as set-ups for my best quips and jokes.

I'd like to recommend this book to you. If you put it in your golf bag, you'll be able to turn any golf disaster into a chuckle. And that would improve your game, wouldn't it?

Bruce Lansky

Golf is a good walk spoiled.
—*Mark Twain*

Golfing: The art of using a flawed swing, a poor stance, and a weak grip to hit a small ball badly towards the wrong hole.
—*Henry Beard and Roy McKie*

A peculiarity of golf is that what you aim at you generally miss.
—*Rex Lardner*

The difference between golf and government
is that in golf you can't improve your lie.
—*Governor George Deukmejian*

The difference between golf and tennis is that
in tennis you want to kill the other player;
in golf you just want to kill yourself.
—*Anonymous*

One of the advantages bowling has over golf
is that you seldom lose a bowling ball.
—*Don Carter, professional bowler*

Golf is like a love affair: if you don't take it
seriously, it's not fun; if you *do* take it
seriously, it breaks your heart.
—*Arnold Daly*

Golf and sex are the only things you can
enjoy without being good at it.
—*Jimmy Demaret*

"I'll be at a seminar on stress."

I'm so distraught about my golf
it's hard to work or think.
My boss suggested, "See a pro;"
my pro said, "See a shrink!"
—Ned Pastor

My psychiatrist prescribed a game of golf
as an antidote to the feelings of euphoria
I experience from time to time.
—*Bruce Lansky*

We learn so many things from golf—
how to suffer, for instance.
—*Bruce Lansky*

Have you ever noticed what
golf spells backwards?
—*Al Bolska*

The tee that's not level,
The ball that is dead,
The fellow who's talking,
The slowpokes ahead,

The fairway that's soggy,
The place of the cup,
The tree needing trimming,
The wind that comes up,

The shaft that is crooked,
The club head that's loose—
It takes little looking
to find an excuse.
                    —Richard Armour

While playing golf today I hit two
good balls. I stepped on a rake.
—*Henny Youngman*

If you drink, don't drive. Don't even putt.
—*Dean Martin*

I've had a good day when
I don't fall out of the cart.
—*Buddy Hackett*

I know I'm getting better at golf
because I'm hitting fewer spectators.
—*Gerald Ford*

We have fifty-one golf courses in Palm Springs.
He (Gerald Ford) never decides which course
he will play until after his first tee shot.
—*Bob Hope*

I deny allegations by Bob Hope
that during my last game
I hit an eagle, a birdie, an elk, and a moose.
—*Gerald Ford*

I'll always remember the day I broke ninety.
I had a few beers in the clubhouse and
was so excited I forgot to play the back nine.
—*Bruce Lansky*

It took me seventeen years to get
three thousand hits in baseball.
I did it in one afternoon on the golf course.
—*Hank Aaron*

God must have loved
the double bogey golfer,
because he made so many of them.
—*Hollis Alpert, Ira Mothner, and*
Harold Schonberg

The only thing in my bag that works
is the bug spray.
—*Bruce Lansky*

Actually, the only time I ever took out
a one iron was to kill a tarantula.
And I took a seven to do that.
—*Jim Murray*

I've thought about buying those new,
long-distance balls, but I wonder—
what's the point of hitting
golf balls even further out of bounds?
—*Bruce Lansky*

I turned down an invitation to play in a best ball tournament because I never play with my best balls. I hate to lose them.

—*Bruce Lansky*

If you don't succeed at first, don't despair. Remember, it takes time to learn to play golf; most players spend their entire lifetime finding out about the game before they give up.

—*Stephen Baker*

Duffer: Well, how do you like my game?
Pro: I suppose it's all right, but I still prefer golf.

—*Wilfred Pickles*

The hardest shot is a mashie at ninety yards from the green, where the ball has to be played against an oak tree, bounces back into a sand trap, hits a stone, bounces on the green, and then rolls into the cup. That shot is so difficult I have only made it once.

—*Zeppo Marx*

In golf, I'm one under. One under a tree, one under a rock, one under a bush . . .

—*Gerry Cheevers*

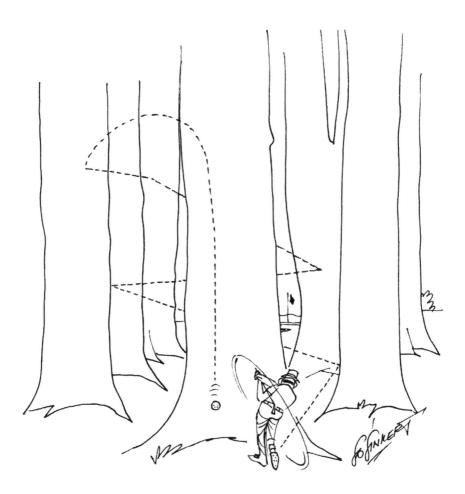

The golf pro is giving a lesson to one of his club members.

"Now, first of all, just take a few swings without hitting the ball," says the pro.

"Hell, I've already mastered that shot," says the member. "I'm paying you to teach me how to hit it."

—Lewis Grizzard

The reason the pro tells you
to keep your head down is
so you can't see him laughing.
—*Phyllis Diller*

A golf pro once gave me some advice
that helped my putting: "Aim low."
—*Bruce Lansky*

If you've played golf for any time at all,
you know by now that taking a lesson
is the quickest and surest way
to ruin your game.
—*Leslie Nielsen and Henry Beard*

Ben (Crenshaw) came to me when he was about eight years old. We cut off a seven iron for him. I showed him a good grip, and we went outside. There was a green about seventy-five yards away. I asked Ben to tee up a ball and hit it onto the green. He did.

Then I said, "Now, let's go to the green and putt the ball into the hole."

Little Ben asked, "If you wanted it in the hole, why didn't you tell me the first time?"

—*Harvey Penick*

You've just one problem.
You stand too close to the ball—
after you've hit it.
—*Sam Snead*

Hacker: What do you think I should do
about my game?
Pro: Well, first I'd take a day off, then
quit for six months, then give it up
entirely.
—*Anonymous*

Nobody ever looked up and saw a good shot.
—*Don Herold*

I found out that all the important lessons
of life are contained in the three rules for
achieving a perfect golf swing:
>   1. Keep your head down
>   2. Follow through
>   3. Be born with money
>   —*P.J. O'Rourke*

Hope: What do you think of my swing?
Palmer: I've seen better swings in
>   a condemned playground.
>   —*Bob Hope and Arnold Palmer*

The more I practice, the luckier I get.
—*Gary Player*

My golf pro said, "Practice makes perfect."
He lied.
—*Bruce Lansky*

I don't need practice. I need a miracle.
—*Bruce Ashworth*

I don't say my golf game is bad,
but if I grew tomatoes they'd come up sliced.
—*Miller Barber*

The best place to refine your swing is,
of course, right out on the practice range. . . .
You will have an opportunity to make
the same mistakes over and over again
so that you no longer have to think
about them, and they become part
of your game.
—*Stephen Baker*

Practice Tee: The place where golfers go
to convert a nasty hook into a wicked slice.
—*Henry Beard and Roy McKie*

I used to go to the driving range to practice
driving without slicing. Now I go to the driving
range to practice slicing without swearing.
—*Bruce Lansky*

The secret of a perfect golf swings
remains a secret.
—*Bruce Lansky*

"Practice makes perfect!"
the pros all decree;
but why does it work
for them and not me?
—Ned Pastor

What a shame to waste those great shots
on the practice tee.
—*Walter Hagen*

My favorite shots are the practice swing
and the conceded putt.
The rest can never be mastered.
—*Lord Robertson*

If I miss one day's practice I know it;
if I miss two days the spectators know it;
and if I miss three days the world knows it.
—*Ben Hogan*

Hacker: This is my first time playing golf.
When do I use my putter?
Caddie: Sometime before dark, I hope.
—*Melvin Helitzer*

Hacker: With my score today I'll never
be able to hold my head up.
Caddie: Why not? You've been doing it
all afternoon.
—*Melvin Helitzer*

27

Golfer: You must be the worst caddie
        in the world.
Caddie: No sir, we couldn't 'ave a
        coincidence like that.
              —Henry Longhurst

Golfer: You perhaps won't believe it, but
        I once did this hole in one.
Caddie: Stroke or day, sir?
              —Ken Dodd

Golfer: I've never played this poorly before.
Caddie: You've played before?
              —Fred Metcalf

Golfer: Caddie, Will you please stop looking
      at your watch all the time?
      It's very distracting.
Caddie: It's not my watch, sir.
      It's my compass.
        —Fred Metcalf

Hacker: Any ideas on how I can cut about
      ten strokes off my score?
Caddie: Yes, quit on seventeen.
        —Melvin Helitzer

Marge: I had to call you. Walter has left me.
Helen: Don't worry. He's left you before,
but he always comes back.
Marge: Not this time. He took his golf clubs.
—*Bruce Lansky*

First Golfer: I got some new golf clubs
for my wife.
Second Golfer: Gee, that's great! I wish
I could make a trade like that!
—*Anonymous*

Golfer (to members ahead): Pardon, but
would you mind if I played through?
I've just heard that my wife
has been taken seriously ill.
—*Lewis and Faye Copeland*

Wife: I know it's too much to expect,
but if you ever spent a Sunday
with me instead of playing golf,
I think I'd drop dead.
Husband: Bribery will get you nowhere.
—*Anonymous*

Eric: My wife says if I don't give up golf
she'll leave me.
Ernie: That's terrible.
Eric: I know, I'm really gonna miss her.
—*Eric Morecambe and Ernie Wise*

You can make a lot of money in this game.
Just ask my ex-wives. Both of them are
so rich that neither of their husbands work.
—*Lee Trevino*

My ex-wife has never broken 150.
I wish she'd stop telling people I taught her
how to play golf.
—*Bruce Lansky*

"All right children, your father will now tell us about his golf game today in one ten-second sound bite."

Honey, do you have anything to say
before the golf season starts?
—*Robert E. Zorn*

My wife doesn't care what I do when I'm away,
as long as I don't have a good time.
—*Lee Trevino*

Wife: You think so much of your golf
game you don't even remember
when we were married.
Husband: Of course I do, my dear. It was the
day I sank that thirty-foot putt.
—*Geoffrey Mattson*

By the time a man can afford
to lose a golf ball,
he can't hit it that far.
—*Lewis Grizzard*

That's the easiest sixty-nine I ever made.
—*Walter Hagen, on turning sixty-nine*

I don't think I'll live long enough
to shoot my age.
I'm lucky to shoot my weight.
—*Bruce Lansky*

Now that I am sixty-nine
but not quite yet a sage,
I just have one ambition left,
and that's to shoot my age.

—Ned Pastor

The great thing about starting golf
in your forties is that you *can* start
golf in your forties. You can start other
things in your forties but generally
your wife makes you stop them,
as Bill Clinton found out.
—*P.J. O'Rourke*

At my stage of life the greatest thrill
a guy gets is sinking a forty-foot putt.
—*Tip O'Neill*

When you get up there in years,
the fairways get longer
and the holes get smaller.
—*Bobby Locke*

The older I get, the harder it is
to remember all the penalty strokes.
—*Bruce Lansky*

Any game where a man sixty can beat
a man thirty ain't no game.
—*Burt Shotten*

If it goes right, it's a slice.
If it goes left, it's a hook.
If it goes straight, it's a miracle.
—*T-shirt*

Murray: Have I got a shot to the green?
Caddie: Mr. Murray, I'd say you have several shots to the green.
—*Jan Murray*

Player: Can I reach it with a five iron?
Caddie: Eventually.
—*John Adams*

"...bad slice?"

On the second tee
It's all right with me
If I start my old topping and botching;
But give me a long one,
A straight one, a strong one,
On the first, when so many are watching.
—Richard Armour

It's easy to keep your drives on the fairway,
as long as you don't care which one.
—*Bruce Lansky*

What goes up must come down.
But don't expect it to come down
where you can find it.
—*Lily Tomlin*

If I had cleared the trees and drove the green,
it would've been a great tee shot.
—*Sam Snead*

"Reckless driving—what about you?"

Something tells me
my swing is all wrong
when I tend to hit drives
that are higher than long.
—Ned Pastor

In case of a thunderstorm, stand in the
middle of the fairway and hold up a one iron.
Not even God can hit a one iron.

—*Lee Trevino*

When I was a kid, my father taught me
the best way to handle a strong wind.
Stay in the clubhouse.

—*Bruce Lansky*

Here in Minnesota we temporarily suspend winter rules on the Fourth of July.
—*Bruce Lansky*

I played as much golf as I could
in North Dakota,
but summer up there is pretty short.
It usually falls on Tuesday.
—*Mike Morley*

The woods are full of long hitters.
—*Harvey Penick*

I'm hitting the woods just great.
But I'm having a terrible time
getting out of them.
—*Harry Toscano*

First Golfer: I hit so many balls into the
woods I lost all my balls.
Second Golfer: That's nothing. I hit so many
balls into the woods I lost my caddie.
—*Bruce Lansky*

A ball will always come to rest
halfway down a hill, unless there is sand
or water at the bottom.
—*Henry Beard*

There's an old saying: If a man comes home
with sand in his cuffs and cockleburs
in his pants, don't ask him what he shot.
—*Sam Snead*

You're supposed to rake the sand smooth
in the bunker after you're finished,
but when I get through with a bunker,
it takes hours. It's like cleaning up
after a hurricane.
—*Bruce Lansky*

To whiff a bunker shot can make
a golfer feel like quite a sap—
then absolutely hopeless when
he blasts into another trap.

—Ned Pastor

"If there's any water we'll know in a sec."

What's the point of washing off your ball
when teeing off on a water hole?
—*Bruce Lansky*

Two balls in the water. By God, I've got a good
mind to jump in and make it four!
—*Simon Hobday*

Golfer: Would you mind wading into the
        pond and retrieving my ball?
Caddie: Why?
Golfer: It's my lucky ball.
—*Bruce Lansky*

53

A duffer fell into a water hazard and screamed, "Help, I'm drowning."

"Don't worry. You'll never drown," yelled his partner, "You can't keep your head down."

—Bruce Lansky

Once when I was golfing in Georgia
I hooked the ball into the swamp.
I went in after it and found an alligator
wearing a shirt with a picture
of a little golfer on it.

—Buddy Hackett

A guy was golfing with a priest. They were on the tenth tee. The guy missed a three-foot putt and said, "God damn it, I missed." The priest told him not to use vulgar language on the course.

On the next hole the guy missed a two-foot putt and said, "God damn it, I missed." The priest told him that if he used vulgar language on the course again, God would strike him down with a lightning bolt and kill him.

Then on the next hole the guy missed a one-foot putt and said, "God damn it, I missed." All of a sudden a lightning bolt came down and killed the priest. From the clouds the guy heard, "God damn it, I missed."

—*Anonymous*

One day a priest was playing golf on the fabled Muirfield course in Scotland. He hit a tee shot into a deep fairway bunker and found his ball buried in sand at the base of a bunker wall four feet high. The priest looked at his ball, turned his face to heaven, and said, "God help me." Then he looked back at the ball, turned again toward heaven, and added, "And, God, don't send Jesus. This is no shot for a boy!"

—Lewis Grizzard

A priest was about to tee off over a lake on a par three hole. Because he was not confident that he could carry the water, he teed up an old ball, and just as he was about to hit, a voice from above said, "Put down a new ball." So he changed to a new ball and was about to hit when the voice said, "Take a practice swing." The priest took a practice swing and again stepped up to the ball, only to hear the voice say, "Put down the old ball."

—*Anonymous*

Priest: I wonder if it would help if I prayed
before I teed off.
Caddie: Only if you pray with your head down.
—*Melvin Helitzer*

Actually, the Lord answers my prayers
everywhere except on the course.
—*Billy Graham*

There was a thunderous crack (of lightning)
like cannon fire and suddenly I was lifted
a foot and a half off the ground. . . .
Damn, I thought to myself, this is
a helluva penalty for slow play.
—*Lee Trevino*

"Caddie, what do you suggest I use for this shot?"

Vicar to partner, chidingly: I have observed
that the best golfers are not
addicted to bad language.
His partner: Of course not—what the hell
do they have to swear about?
—*Geoffrey Mattson*

Golf is a game of expletives not deleted.
—*Dr. Irving I. Gladstone*

Follow-through: The part of the swing
that takes place after the ball has been hit,
but before the club has been thrown.
—*Henry Beard and Roy McKie*

I've thrown a few clubs in my day. In fact,
I guess at one time or another I held
distance records for every club in the bag.
—*Tommy Bolt*

If you are going to throw a club, it is
important to throw it ahead of you, down the
fairway, so you don't have to waste energy
going back to pick it up.
—*Tommy Bolt*

The most exquisitely satisfying act in the world of golf is that of throwing a club. The full backswing, the delayed wrist action, the flowing follow-through, followed by that unique whirring sound, reminiscent only of a passing flock of starlings, are without parallel in sport.

—*Henry Longurst*

I don't enjoy playing video golf because there's nothing to throw.

—*Paul Azinger*

*"Next time you throw your golf clubs
into a ravine let go of them first!"*

Golfer at confession: I have a confession to make.
I used the Lord's name in vain on the golf
course.

Priest: You know, I'm a golfer too. I'd like to hear
about it.

Golfer: Well, my opponent drove the first shot right
up the middle of the fairway. I shanked mine
into the rough.

Priest: I'm sorry to hear that. Is that when you took
the Lord's name in vain?

Golfer: No Father, I've got a lot of confidence in my
long irons. My opponent hit a seven iron
onto the green. I hit a terrific four iron that
bounced over the green and rolled into a
bunker.

Priest: I'm sorry to hear that. Is that when you took the Lord's name in vain?

Golfer: No Father. I've got a lot of confidence in my wedge. My opponent putted to within a yard of the cup. I blasted out of the bunker. The ball hit the pin and stopped rolling just two feet from the cup.

Priest: Jesus Christ! Don't tell me you blew the putt.

—Bruce Lansky

I may be the only golfer never to have broken
a single putter, if you don't count the one
I twisted and threw into a bush.
—*Thomas Boswell*

Mr. Byers and I played terribly.
He was a veteran and I was a youngster,
but we expressed our feelings in exactly the
same way. When we missed a shot, we threw
the club away. I think the main reason I beat
him was because he ran out of clubs first.
—*Bobby Jones*

Why am I using a new putter? Because the old one didn't float too well.
—*Craig Stadler*

Ninety percent of the putts that fall short don't go in.
—*Yogi Berra*

Half of golf is fun, the other half is putting.
—*Peter Dobereiner*

Downhill putts break more.
Uphill putts break less.
No putt ever breaks
exactly as I guess.
　　　—*Timothy Tocher*

Never putt until the cup stops moving.
—Bruce Lansky

**These greens are so fast I have to hold
my putter over the ball and hit it
with the shadow.**
—Sam Snead

**The way I putted, I must've been reading
the greens in Spanish and putting them
in English.**
—Homero Blancas

I was lying ten and had a thirty-five-foot
putt. I whispered over my shoulder:
"How does this one break?"
And my caddie said, "Who cares?"
—*Jack Lemmon*

Tap-in: A putt short enough
to miss one-handed.
—*Henry Beard and Roy McKie*

Gimme: An agreement between two losers
who can't putt.
—*Jim Bishop*

*"I know the golf course is a block away!
Don't rub it in!"*

Talking to a golf ball won't do you any good.
Unless you do it while your opponent
is teeing off.
—*Bruce Lansky*

Go ahead and putt. You're not interrupting
my conversation.
—*Robert E. Zorn*

It is a serious breach of etiquette to point
out the flaws in your opponent's swing—
unless you are behind.
—*Bruce Lansky*

New Member: How does one meet new people at this club?

Old Member: Try picking up the wrong golf ball.

—*Anonymous*

A: Why aren't you playing golf with the colonel?

B: Would you play golf with someone who curses at every shot, cheats in the bunkers, and enters false scores on his cards?

A: Certainly not.

B: Neither will the colonel.

—*Freddie Oliver*

The divot is a piece of sod
That ought to be replaced and trod
Upon by golfing gentlemen,
And thus allowed to grow again.

For otherwise it leaves a spot
Scooped out and bare, where, like as not,
If there is justice, by and by
The divoteer's own ball will lie.

—Richard Armour

Manager: I'm sorry, sir, we have no time open on the course today.

Golfer: Wait a minute, what if Arnold Palmer and Jack Nicklaus showed up? I'm sure you'd find a starting time for them.

Manager: Of course we would, sir.

Golfer: Well, I happen to know they're not coming, so we'll take their time.

—Anonymous

At Jinja there is both a hotel and golf
course. The latter is, I believe, the only course
in the world which posts a special rule
that the player may remove his ball
from hippopotamus footprints.
—*Evelyn Waugh*

If a ball comes to rest in dangerous proximity
to a hippopotamus or crocodile, another ball
may be dropped at a safe distance, no nearer
the hole, without penalty.
—*Local rule, Nyanza Club,*
British East Africa, 1950

"These? They're the Rules of Golf!"

Thou shalt not use profanity; thou shalt not covet thy neighbor's putter; thou shalt not steal thy neighbor's ball; thou shalt not bear false witness in the final tally.
—*Ground rules, clergymen's tournament*

A sign on a Scottish golf course reads as follows: "Members will refrain from picking up lost balls until they have stopped rolling."
—*Lewis and Faye Copeland*

Golf has more rules than any other game, because golf has more cheaters than any other game.
—*Bruce Lansky*

You know the old rule. He who have fastest
cart never have to play bad lie.
—*Mickey Mantle*

The First Rule of Golf: It ain't a stroke
if no one else saw it.
—*Jim Becker, Andy Mayer, and Rick Wolff*

At my age I have trouble remembering all the
official rules. So, I keep it simple. If I lose a
ball I add a stroke. If I find a ball I deduct a
stroke. I often play with my dog, a golden
retriever, and hit twenty or thirty under par.
People ask me what my handicap is.
I reply: "With or without my dog?"
—*Bruce Lansky*

Golf is a game in which you yell "fore,"
shoot six, and write down five.
—*Paul Harvey*

If there are several caddies waiting around
for an assignment, I ask them all to add
forty-seven plus fifty-four. Then I choose
the one with the lowest answer.
—*Bruce Lansky*

There is no surer nor [more] painful way
to learn a rule than to be penalized once
for breaking it.
—*Tom Watson*

One time at Chattanooga I hit a real pretty iron to the green, and danged if my ball didn't hit a bobwhite in the air and knock it dead. My ball stopped about a foot from the cup and I knocked it in. Only time I ever made two birdies on the same hole.

—*Sam Snead*

Do you know what it means to open up your scorecard and see pars or birdies on every hole? It means you've got the wrong scorecard.

—*Bruce Lansky*

Like Audubon of avian fame,
I spend long hours at this game,
where it is good and not illegal
to shoot a birdie or an eagle.

—Lois Muehl

It is harder to cut strokes from your score
than it is to add strokes to your
opponent's score.
—*Bruce Lansky*

Some golfers fantasize about playing
in a foursome with Arnold Palmer, Jack
Nicklaus, and Sam Snead. The way I hit
I'd rather play in a foursome with Helen Keller,
Ray Charles, and Stevie Wonder.
—*Bruce Lansky*

Mulligan: It's often necessary to hit a second
shot to really appreciate the first one.
—*Henry Beard*

"...Here's a score for you. I had a triple mulligan and a birdie..."

Golf is a game in which the ball always lies
poorly and the player well.

—*Anonymous*

Lie: 1. Where the ball comes to rest
after being hit by a golfer.
2. The number of strokes it took to get
it there, as reported by that golfer.

—*Henry Beard and Roy McKie*

On a recent survey, 80 percent of golfers admitted cheating. The other 20 percent lied.
—*Bruce Lansky*

You have to admit that golfers' scorecards are relatively honest. Relative to their income tax forms.
—*Bruce Lansky*

I used to play golf with a guy who cheated so badly that he once had a hole-in-one and wrote down zero on his scorecard.
—*Bob Bruce*

Vice President Spiro Agnew can't cheat
on his score—because all you have to do
is look back down the fairway
and count the wounded.
—*Bob Hope*

I'm a nineteen and I think Bob's about
nineteen, but he cheats more than I do.
—*Dolores Hope*

What some people will do for an advantage!
I knew a guy who had a sex-change operation
so he could play golf from the ladies' tees.
—*Anonymous*

I have a tip that can take five strokes off
anyone's golf game. It's called an eraser.
—*Arnold Palmer*

Did you ever stop and think why the pencils
they give out with scorecards
don't have erasers?
—*Bruce Lansky*

You don't know what pressure is
until you play for five bucks with only two
in your pocket.
—*Lee Trevino*

There is no such thing as a friendly wager.
—*Henry Beard*

If you break one hundred, watch your golf.
If you break eighty, watch your business.
—*Joey Adams*

A golf match is a test of your skill
against your opponent's luck.
—*Henry Beard*

The main problem with keeping your eye
on the ball is you have to take your eye
off your opponent
—*Bruce Lansky*

I'm only scared of three things—lightning,
a side-hill putt, and Ben Hogan.
—*Sam Snead*

He can draw a ball or fade it
and does either with aplomb;
so beware of foolish wagers
or you'll wind up broke and glum.

He can hook a ball or slice it,
then adopt a doleful mien;
but beware of his approaches,
for they seldom miss the green.

Since he's deadly from a bunker
and uncanny from the rough,
best beware of extra presses—
he will win them sure enough.

If you need two feet for birdie
while his ball is twenty shy,
chances are that when he holes it,
you'll miss yours and wonder why.

Yes, beware the friendly hustler—
don't be swayed by pride or whim;
just remember that your money's
better off with you than him!

—Ned Pastor

My worst day on the golf course still beats my best day in the office.
—*John Hallisey*

Your financial cost can best be figured out when you realize that if you were to devote the same time and energy to business instead of golf, you would be a millionaire in approximately six weeks.
—*Buddy Hackett*

"I'm going to make this short..."

Someone once told me that there's more
to life than golf. I think it was my ex-wife.
—*Bruce Lansky*

It really doesn't matter if there's life
after death if there isn't golf after death.
—*Bruce Lansky*

I'm very lucky. If it wasn't for golf I don't know
what I'd be doing. If my IQ had been two
points lower, I'd have been a plant somewhere.
—*Lee Trevino*

Weight distributed,
Free from strain,
Divot replaced,
Familiar terrain,
Straight left arm,
Unmoving head—
Here lies the golfer,
Cold and dead.
   —Richard Armour

"That way he doesn't mind taking out the garbage."

A woman I know is engaged to a real golf nut.
They're supposed to get married
next Saturday . . . but only if it rains.
—*Cindy Garner*

Golf is a terrible game. I'm glad I don't have
to play again until tomorrow.
—*Anonymous*

My golf club sells postcards so golfers can
let their families know where they are.
—*Bruce Lansky*

Two avid golfers were sitting in the clubhouse. One said to his friend, "I'm sorry to hear that your uncle passed away last week. I understand it was while you two were playing golf. I hear you carried him all the way back to the clubhouse. That must have been very hard for you considering he weighed over two hundred pounds."

"Oh, carrying him wasn't that hard," said his friend, sadly. "The difficult part was putting him down . . . and then picking him up again after each stroke."

—Roger Bates

"Do you think there's golf in heaven?" said one old man to another.

"I sure hope so," said the second. "I tell you what. Whoever dies first will come back and tell the other."

Three weeks later, the first fellow died. Shortly thereafter, his friend heard his voice as he lay in bed.

"Bill, I've come back to tell you about heaven."

"Is there golf there?" the second man asked.

"Well, I've got good news and bad news. The good news is there is golf in heaven, and everybody shoots par."

"So what's the bad news?"

"The bad news is you've got a tee time next Tuesday."

—*Lewis Grizzard*

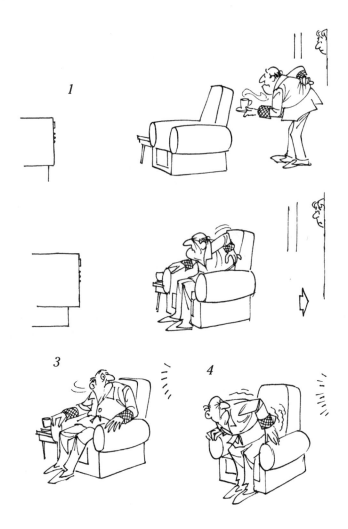

INDEX

Order Form

Qty.	Title	Author	Order #	Unit Cost	Total
	Age Happens	Lansky, B.	4025	$7.00	
	Baby Name Personality Survey	Lansky/Sinrod	1270	$8.00	
	Best Baby Shower Book	Cooke, C.	1239	$7.00	
	Best Party Book	Warner, P.	6089	$8.00	
	Best Wedding Shower Book	Cooke, C.	6059	$7.00	
	Dads Say the Dumbest Things!	Lansky/Jones	4220	$6.00	
	Familiarity Breeds Children	Lansky, B.	4015	$7.00	
	For Better And For Worse	Lansky, B.	4000	$6.00	
	Golf: It's Just a Game	Lansky, B.	4035	$7.00	
	Grandma Knows Best	McBride, M.	4009	$6.00	
	How to Survive Your 40th Birthday	Dodds, B.	4260	$6.00	
	If We'd Wanted Quiet/Poems for Parents	Lansky, B.	3505	$12.00	
	Joy of Grandparenting	Sherins/Holleman	3502	$7.00	
	Joy of Marriage	Dodds, M. & B.	3504	$7.00	
	Joy of Parenthood	Blaustone, J.	3500	$6.00	
	Moms Say the Funniest Things!	Lansky, B.	4280	$6.00	
				Subtotal	
			Shipping and Handling (see below)		
			MN residents add 6.5% sales tax		
				Total	

YES! Please send me the books indicated above. Add $2.00 shipping and handling for the first book and 50¢ for each additional book. Add $2.50 to total for books shipped to Canada. Overseas postage will be billed. Allow up to four weeks for delivery. Send check or money order payable to Meadowbrook Press. No cash or COD's, please. Prices subject to change without notice. **Quantity discounts available upon request.**
Send book(s) to:

Name _____ Address _____

City _____ State ____ Zip _____ Telephone (_____) _____

P.O. number (if necessary) _____ Payment via: ❑ Check or money order payable to Meadowbrook Press

Amount enclosed $ _____ ❑ Visa ❑ MasterCard (for orders over $10.00 only)

Account # _____ Signature _____ Exp. Date _____

A *FREE* Meadowbrook Press catalog is available upon request.

Mail to: Meadowbrook, Inc.
18318 Minnetonka Boulevard, Deephaven, MN 55391

(612) 473-5400   Toll-Free 1-800-338-2232   Fax (612) 475-0736